Special <u>FREE</u> Bonus Gift for <u>YOU!</u>

To help you achieve more success, there are
FREE BONUS RESOURCES for you at:

YourBonusGift.com

FREE SOCIAL MEDIA CONTENT PLUS
A FREE SOCIAL MEDIA TRAINING DAY VIDEO

FREE $1997 VALUE

Get started now at
YourBonusGift.com

THE

HOWS AND WHYS OF

SOCIAL MEDIA

THE
HOWS AND
WHYS OF
SOCIAL MEDIA

The Marketing Checklist 3

Hank and Sharyn Yuloff

Naked Book Publishing

Contents

THE SECRETS of SOCIAL MEDIA to BUILD BUSINESS

"Share This Book"

Retail
$14.95

Special Quantity Discounts

5-20 Books	$13.95
21-99 Books	$11.50
100-499 Books	$10.25
500-999 Books	$8.95
1000+ Books	$6.95

To Place Your Order Contact:
(800)705-4265
Info@YuloffCreative.com
www.Yuloff Creative .com

Introduction

When we are asked to speak to business people in groups as small as ten to groups in the hundreds, the most popular topics have to do with social media. Whether it is on the basic level or to more advanced audiences, there is a hunger for easy-to-understand information on how to use social media to market a business.

Our most active audiences are those in our social media marketing sessions, with so many hands raised with questions. In fact, we usually ask for everyone to hold their question until the end and we will chat with them individually. Many of those questions begin with the phrase, "I heard that . . . ." And then they proceed to share something that had to be a wild guess by someone who was confused with how to use this medium to promote a business.

Using social media for business purposes is a different animal from how we can use social media for personal purposes to connect with family and friends. To use a sports analogy, it's like the difference between a major league baseball pitcher's curveball and a high school pitcher beginning to experiment with her off-speed pitches.

The most often-asked question when we speak to associations and other groups is, "How do I know what to post on social media? What does my audience want to see?" The simplest answer is, "be interesting." Even as a business, you should treat social media as your backyard barbeque party. It is a *social* interaction. Business discussions are saved until after we get to know each other a little more; after having shared a soda and been in line together scooping potato salad onto our plates while chatting about things we have in common.

This book is an attempt to help you answer some of the most obvious questions that we receive, and as a bonus, give you enough social media memes for a business to be able to post one a day for each day of the work week for fifty-two weeks. You can find that information at www.YourBonusGift.com.

We will continue to create and add more content at that site so the further past the publication date we travel together, the more valuable your purchase of this book will have become.

As an additional bonus, we have included the videos from a day-long social media class we taught at our home office in a room we call "The War Room" where we put together the marketing plans for small business owners who become private coaching clients. That social media training day is part of our online do-it-yourself *with coaching* marketing program called The Small Business Marketing Plan (details at www.TheSmallBusinessMarketingPlan. com).

We thank you for purchasing this book! We appreciate your business and look forward to helping your small business grow larger.

With appreciation,
Sharyn and Hank Yuloff
www.YuloffCreative.com

1

The Myths of Social Media

First, let's take care of four myths about social media: It's a silver bullet; it's easy; it takes very little time; and you must use, and be an expert in, all the different platforms.

- **It's a silver bullet:** Social media is just one of the marketing tactics you will use for your marketing.

- **It's easy:** While it's certainly not rocket science, it does take some practice engaging with your ideal clients to perfect your messaging.

- **It takes very little time:** It takes time to build up your audience and then convert that audience into paying clients. It happens a little bit every day, not all at once.

- **You must use, and be an expert in, all the different platforms:** Start with the platform that your ideal client is likely to use. Since almost everyone is either on Facebook or living with someone who uses Facebook, you'll probably want to start there. Perfect Facebook and then add other platforms that your ideal client may use after you are comfortable with Facebook.

2

What Are Your Marketing Goals for Social Media?

When you are using any marketing tactic, it is imperative to know what your goals are for the interactions with your target market. This is also true for social media. In addition to your personal goals, here are five goals to achieve in your social media.

1. **Communicate with your clients**. Your clients want to hear from you at least once each day on each platform that you are on. They want to know what you think about what's going on in your industry, how current events are impacting you, and how you think those events will impact them. They want to know what articles you're reading and if you agree with those articles and why you agree.

2. **Maintain a platform that will develop new business.** Gone are the days when we would go to a new vendor without first checking them out online. We want to know why Suzy recommended John to us, rather than to Mike. One of the places we all go to check out a new referral is on their social media pages.

3. **Become a trusted referral source.** You want to be seen as a trusted referral source, not just for your specialty, but for anything someone might need. Be the first person they think of when they have a need. ("Oh, I bet Suzy knows where I can find the best vendor for this need!") To do this, be on the lookout for folks who post that they are looking for a vendor (typically, a tradesperson like a plumber, or a professional like an attorney), then share the information of three different people that could meet their need. I like to highlight my favorite person, then offer two others that they might also like to interview. They might hit it off better with one of the others than my

favorite, for whatever reason. Which also means that your information should be easily accessible so that we can refer you!

4. **Share business tips.** Share information not just from your industry, but also your business experience. You are an entrepreneur after all and have learned some things. You will continue to learn things about business probably every day that you could share on social media.

5. **Our community's amusement.** For an example of this, check out Hank's Facebook profile (and feel free to share any of his posts . . . that's why they are there!). www.fb.com/hankyuloff

Treat your social media like any other marketing tactic. Social media is an online method of communication. How you use social media for your own business depends on your marketing goals.

3

What Platforms Should You Be On?

It's all about demographics and psychographics—that is, who is using the particular platforms and why.

While we have covered the topic of working with different generations in our other books, it's even more important to consider when working with social media. Here is a brief primer on some things to keep in mind when communicating to five different generations:

The **Gen2020** (born after 1997) are growing up with tablet devices and they have an app for everything. They are an optimistic generation with high expectations. They communicate with hand-held communication devices and their preference in making financial decisions will include digital crowd-sourcing. Their attitude toward their career will be a multi-tasking seamless move between organizations and pop-up businesses (short-term venues). The signature product for this generation will be 3-D printing, and the primary platform will be whatever is hot and new. That is how it usually is with the youngest generation.

The most historic event that formed the mindset of the **Millennials** (1977–1997) is the attack of 9/11/01. They are driven by community service and social everything, and they have grown up appreciating the immediacy of change and diversity. They are the first Google and Facebook generation, living their life online with ease and understanding. Their work careers will be characterized by change and fluidity. Their signature products are smart phones and tablets.

The **Gen X** (1965–1976) are independent free agents. They do not expect to work at the same company for a lifetime. They witnessed the fall of the Berlin Wall, which greatly lessoned the fear that had gripped the previous two generations who thought they could be nuked on any day. They saw the invention and rise of the internet, and they watched MTV to see music videos. Where previous generations had seen drugs that would eliminate many diseases, that was not the case with AIDS. They communicate with e-mail and text messages (Sharyn would *love* it if she could do all her business communications that way). Their preference in making financial decisions will include face-to-face options if time permits, but going online is where they do most of their business and manage their personal lives. The signature product of this generation is the personal computer.

The **Boomers** (1946–1964) are so named because of the baby boom, the sharp increase in births, which occurred in the years after World War II. The Boomers were young when the United States landed men on the moon and returned them to Earth safely. It encouraged them to think that all things are possible. They witnessed and were part of the Civil Rights and Women's Rights movements. They are an experimental and innovative generation. They grew up at a time when long distance phone calls were expensive and mobile phones and personal computers did not yet exist. Their first mobile phones were the size of a small suitcase and had to be installed in their cars. They communicate with telephones and their preference in making financial and buying decisions is face-to-face but increasingly includes going online. Their signature product is the television, and gee whiz, *color* television.

The **Traditionalists** (1900–1945) lived through the Great Depression and World War II. They are disciplined in their thinking. They were taught that workplace loyalty was important, meaning that they expected to get a job and stay with that company for their entire work career. When my father was fired from his job at Sav-On Drug for being an organizer of The Guild for Professional Pharmacists (he was the first president), he took it very hard and it effected my parents focus on work for the rest of their lives. This generation grew up with some amazing scientific advances, like vaccines which all but eliminated polio. They communicate with formal letters and their preference in making financial and buying decisions will include face-to-face meetings. The signature product of this generation is the affordable automobile.

The best platforms to use for a particular generation will change over time. But, keep an eye on the generational use of the platforms that you are using to make sure you are reaching your desired audience and that they do not leave you.

4

Paid Advertising on Social Media

We recently ran a post on Facebook that asked if people would be willing to pay for the platform if it was no longer free. Half of the respondents said, "no." Our guess was closer to the answers that we got when we asked that same question at our Small Business Marketing Bootcamps. People would be willing to pay for their most-used platforms if they were sure to get value.

There is a reason that those platforms are free: We are the product they are selling to advertisers. The question is: Should we advertise our businesses on social media? The answer for most businesses is going to be a strong, "Yep—we think so.'"

We go through this extensively with clients, and it takes a while to get it completely right, but here are the basic steps.

The first thing to do is, and always will be, to determine your target market. The more you can narrow it down and decide on the niches you want to do business with, the more effective your advertising will be.

There are two ways to advertise on social media—promoting content and display advertisements with clickable links.

Getting engagement on your organic posts is becoming harder, thanks to platforms continually changing their algorithms. This means that you are going to have to pay if you want to be widely seen. It will depend on your budget, but there are inexpensive ways to dip your toes into the water. The platform you advertise on will mirror where your target market is playing.

When your ads run, you want to watch and see how much response you are getting. The same as if you ran an ad in a newspaper and watched to see how many coupons were redeemed.

Just like print ads, when advertising online, you can run different ads at the same time which will go to distinct geographic or target market areas and see which one does better. This is broadly known as A/B testing. After you run a test, usually a day or so, change one thing in the ad that is performing poorly and see if you can make it perform better than the other one.

You don't only have to run ads only to make sales, you can use them to increase your audience, generate leads, increase the size of your email list, or just get more people to see what you are posting.

It all depends on what your marketing strategy is for social media.

5

Five Things to Never Ever Post on Social Media

1. Never talk about sex. No one cares who one is involved with, and they certainly are not interested any of the drama that can accompany relationships.

2. We don't care about your politics, unless you are considering running, in which case we might actually be interested.

3. Your posts will never change anyone else's religious affiliation. Be sensitive to other religions without trying to convert anyone to yours.

4. Even if they always win, let's not talk about sports teams (unless you or your kids are playing in them).

5. Always *avoid negativity*. The first four items would be seen as negative by someone. So, if you think someone will see your post as negative, don't post it. Call your best friend and vent to them instead!

These suggestions are an attempt to keep your sales funnel as wide open and be as inclusive as possible. However, if it's the professional place where you want to make a stand, put a stake in the ground and spout your beliefs strongly so that you attract those that agree with you.

6

Responding to Negative Posts

Everyone has seen those negative posts. You might be standing in line at your favorite locally-owned coffee shop to get your triple shot of mocha coffee grandalicious. While scrolling through your Facebook feed you see it—Cindy McNegative posts, "I cannot BELIEVE how bad I just got treated by the staff at . . ." and on it goes.

Your first thought? "I am *so* glad that wasn't *my* company Cindy was talking about."

But what if it was? What if one of your new staff members was asked a question he did not know the answer to, stammered a bit, guessed a bit, did not give the right answer, and pissed off a client. The client who woke up this morning on the wrong side of the bed because his dog was barking at the moon most of the night, and when he slid his foot into his $500 leather loafers realized his cat had pooed into his shoe.

And now, you are reading something negative about your company on social media. So, what are you going to do about it? Here is the best thing I can tell you: *Do not ignore it.*

And since you are not going to ignore it, here is the 3-step program we use at Yuloff Creative Marketing Solutions to bail out your marketing:

Step 1: Take a deep breath and a step back. They're attacking your brand, not *you*. Do not take it personally or you could make it worse.

Step 2: Identify what their motivation was for posting the negative comment. Do they want a reaction? Do they want you to react badly? Do they want a problem solved?

Step 3: Agree, Disarm, Solve. "We are sorry you had this occur. We can see your point because . . . ." (Tell them why.) "We would like to resolve this by . . ." (*Solve the problem.*)

I know, eating crow when it is not your fault is *really* hard. I understand. But as your Chief Marketing Officer, I am telling you that you just need to do it.

It's now normal for customer service to be handled on social media, so we have to adapt and use it to our brand's advantage. In fact, there are a lot of companies who have separate Twitter accounts for their customer service departments. You can too.

Do you need some help with setting up your customer service social media program? Connect with us at www.Facebook.com/YuloffCreative and we will talk about it.

7

What's the Biggest Mistake People Make on Social Media? The 80/20 Rule

Social media is rather like going to a backyard barbecue. People are hanging around, getting to know each other, having a cold beverage and a warm sandwich.

If an insurance agent (one who is brand new and doesn't know any better) shows up in a suit instead of a t-shirt, shorts, and flip-flops, she would seem out of place, right? What would be your reaction? If you are like most people in this situation, they would get as far away from Ingrid Insurance Agent as possible.

Consider your personal social media page a Saturday afternoon event in your friend's back yard. People do not want to be sold at the barbecue and they don't really want to be sold on your page. That does not mean you cannot include any business on your page—after all, when you meet someone in the backyard, you *do* ask other guests what they do for a living, right?

So here is the rule of thumb: No more than 20% of the posts on your personal page should be about business.

Similarly, no more than 20% of the posts on your business/fan/like page should be about personal things like lunch . . . or your cats . . . or how you shared your lunch with your cats.

Here is a great way to use the two pages together. Let's say you wrote a new blog post. After you publish it on your website, take the link and post it on your business page. *Then* you can hit the *share* button on that page and post it to your personal page. The idea is to link it back to your website. Lead them by the hand to the place you want them to go—your website.

8

Differences Between the Types of Facebook Pages

So, what's the difference between a personal profile and a business page?

You must start with a personal profile. That's the one you're probably most used to seeing. Your profile is where all your friends see what you are up to and what you're thinking about.

Your business page is the one you build from your profile where your ideal clients Like your business. The big difference between the two is that you can see a lot of statistics, what Facebook calls "Insights" on your business page.

On the business page you can see the demographics of who visits your page: gender, age, location, etc. You can also see what types of posts they engage with the most on your page. Do they prefer your memes? Your videos? Your blog posts?

9

Different Types of Posts

Once you have those pages, here are the five types of posts:

- **Memes**. You know . . . those square images you see with words on them. Check out Hank's personal profile for loads of examples: www.fb.com/hankyuloff

- **Questions**. Although we were all raised to ask open-ended questions to get people talking about themselves, this typically doesn't work on social media. Everyone is scanning so quickly, that just hitting the Like button is about all one can handle. However, for more of your posts to be seen, you must encourage engagement. The best way to do this is to only offer Yes or No questions.

- **Text**. These are what we've become most accustomed to—those posts that are typed text questions/comments/thoughts.

- **Video**. According to Facebook VP Nicola Mendelsohn in 2016, our Facebook newsfeed will be all video by 2021. This is because most engagement (Likes, Comments, and Shares) occur on video posts.

- **Link**. This is what happens when you share your blog post, other articles, and YouTube videos. They are links back to the original media.

10

Seven Tips to Make Your Social Media Video More Effective

First, why use video at all?

- It drastically improves your speaking and presentation skills.
- Your show can be uploaded to iTunes.
- You can turn your radio shows into products or a book.
- To make sure your guests post the link, and other information about your show on their social media.

You can even do shows on location to switch things up a bit and include others. But remember, even if you are only doing a podcast, it's important that you still are consistent on the time and day.

Now on to the tips:

1. Like your blog, create a compelling title for your video, including key words that people would use to search out your page.

2. Be yourself. When people hire you, they are going to expect the same person they saw on the video.

3. Promote the event in advance, as you would if it was a webinar.

4. Promote the event on other social media channels after it's been uploaded to YouTube.

5. Keep your eye on the comments, as this is the way your will attendees communicate with you.

6. Use it for trainings, sharing the link with your client so that they can review anything they may have missed during your chat.

7. Practice shooting video with whichever camera you are using to capture your message. There are many devices which capture video, so

whichever one you use, get good at using it. What will always be most important is the message that you are delivering to your target markets.

11

Six Tips for More Effective Tweets

1. Emphasize the need for urgency.

2. Express discounts in percentages.

3. Remember, newer is better.

4. #Always #Avoid #Distracting #Hashtags

5. Keep it short and sweet. (Practice to see *how few* of those 280 characters you can use.)

6. Spark interest by asking a question. (It's hard to have a conversation on Twitter *but* the human mind has a hard time *not* answering a question. Try it:
   What is your favorite color?
   What is your favorite movie?
   See? Pretty cool, huh? Oh, there went *another* question.

And a 7th bonus tip: Become President of the United States . . . *everyone* will at least *hear* about what you are tweeting.

12

Ten Tips to Make Your Instagram Account More Effective

1. Create a template for your posts so that the photos in your feed are all similarly branded.

2. Upload at least nine of your branded photos before you start following others so that they have nine images to look at when they go to see who followed them and before they consider following you back.

3. Make sure your account is *not* set to private (no one can find you that way and if you comment or follow on others' posts, they will go to your account and see it's private and won't have any information on why they should follow you).

4. Create a list of hashtags (you can use up to thirty) in a notes app on your phone (we use Evernote) so that you can copy and paste them easily into the first comment on your post.

5. Don't post the hashtags into the caption field. Keep your initial post clean of hashtags.

6. Link your account to Facebook, Twitter, Tumbler, etc., so that you extend your reach.

7. Like and Comment on others' posts (it will encourage them to do the same for you).

8. When folks comment on your posts, reply to those comments promptly!

9. Build your community by occasionally sharing another's post using a re-sharing app (we use the Repost app, but there are others).

10. Although you can upload videos, as well, most users won't watch them. Test it out with your audience because it's really all about them, not general information.

13

How to Make All Your Posts Go Viral

Wow, this one is simple. All you must do is click the "viral" button that each social media platform has on their profile. *(*Insert blank stare here.*)*

Boy, if our clients would blog every time they asked us to make their posts go viral, we would never have to remind them to blog.

Guess what? There is no simple way you can guarantee that your any of your social posts (or blogs) will go viral and become the next "Momma Panda Scared by Sneezing Baby Panda" (Google it). Here are a few tips which may help.

- Video is more likely to go viral than posts that contain only words.

- Strong emotional appeals help—laughter, tears, family, kids doing something cute (Google "Charlie Bit My Finger").

- It must be very easy to understand, and it must make people want to share it.

- Make them want to spread awareness of something.

- Keep it positive or uplifting. Things that make us feel good about ourselves will make people want to share it with others.

- It should be easy to find. Don't hide it on an inside page of your website. Or if you do, share it on your social media pages.

- Don't forget to have it publicize your company while you are at it.

- Ideally, there would be a way to connect it back to you so that people can have a conversation with you.

14

How Often Should You Post?

That is a great question. It is the most often-asked question we face when we work with clients on their marketing. Here is the short answer: At least once each day on every platform you are on consistently.

Here is the longer answer: Watch your Insights. Post as often as you can do so consistently without not losing your audience. Watch those Insights to see when your largest audience is viewing your page.

We have people tell us all the time that to post every day is, "so very hard, oh my goodness." Here is just a little tough love: You're just going to have to get over that little hurdle and post away.

We recommend that you post far more often, at least twice a day. Remember that people are reading their social media newsfeeds when they have a few minutes to spare: in line at the store, when they are sitting at a red light, while they are waiting for their child to come out of school, while they are waiting for their parent to pick them up, or perhaps when they are brushing their teeth. This means that they are only scrolling back and looking at the last few hours of posts. If you are not there every few hours, they will go a long time without hearing from you.

There are several apps which you can use to post when you are not in front of the computer and that will make your job a lot easier. For up-to-date suggestions on our favorite apps, connect with us on our Creative Social Media pages.

15

I Don't Have Time

"But Hank and Sharyn, I don't have the time to do all that social media stuff. I'm busy." (In other words, they don't know what to post, they need help, and they are letting their niece who just got out of college run their social media). "Should I hire someone to do it for me?"

Our clients spend more time asking that question than it would take if they would just sit down and blog. This is more of a case of anticipated overwhelm than actual overwhelm.

So, do you need to hire someone? Maybe.

If your company does not include staff with the expertise to put together a social media campaign, then hiring an expert might be a good idea. A professional may have knowledge you don't and that can help you be more effective.

If you *do* hire someone, however, do *not* just give them the keys to the kingdom and consider it handled. They do not know your brand as well as you do and if left on their own, without guidance, your social media might take a wrong turn. In fact, if the person you hire *wants* to take complete control, they are the wrong person. When we work with clients and run their social media for them, we are in very regular contact to ensure their brand is being effectively communicated.

It's the same with someone on staff. Do not make them the administrator. Keep that for yourself. Remember, it's *your* car. *you* paid for it. You should be the only one who can register it, drive it, and know where it's parked at night.

16

Trends at the Time of This Writing

1. Facebook is the biggest player on the block. Every generation is using it. We suggest to our clients that they become well versed in this platform and then choose one other platform that their largest target market is using.

2. Increasingly, video is being seen on each platform. This trend began when Google bought YouTube and began promoting videos on search engines. In fact, they are the two largest places where people seek answers.

3. Even if you are not on a platform, it makes sense to reserve your spot on the platform. In the future it might turn into something you need.

4. Be consistent with the names you use on each platform. When getting onto social media, check each of the major sites to ensure your desired name is available on each one. This makes it easier for your audience to find you. It also makes tagging across platforms easier.

5. In our promotional product business, people always ask us, "What are the best products to use?" Our answer to that question is the same as the question, "How do I get a larger audience." If you want a larger audience, create content that is useful and is needed by them. When one is spending time on social media they are giving up a very useful resource—time. The biggest excuse we hear about why people don't use social media is that they don't have time. *So,* if someone is

scanning through different platforms, we want to give them content that they will find exciting, useful, and fulfilling.

6. People always want to know, "What is the best time to post?" The easy answer: There is no best time. It depends on the platforms you use and when your audience is checking those platforms. Most business pages have an Insights page where you can check these details. Keep in mind that sometimes it is takes a while until you have posted enough to check the engagement rates.

17

Epilogue

During one of our events when Hank wants to give you the bottom line answer to a complicated question, he says "Here's the thing . . ."

So, regarding social media, what is most important to consider? Here's the thing and it's a three-part formula.

1. Remember that a basic rule of marketing is to never create your marketing message without knowing *exactly* who you are creating it for.

2. If you have read this book, you are a business person so remember to always look at social media through a business person's eyes with that focus turned *towards increasing your business*. **Therefore . . .**

3. All your business posts should be designed towards speaking to and capturing the attention of your target markets. Do you have more than one target market? Then design different posts for each of them and understand and accept that those posts will also capture some business from your other targets.

There you go. Thank you for reading this book and remember that if you have questions, we are very easy to find on, where else, social media.

Special <u>FREE</u> Bonus Gift for <u>YOU!</u>

To help you achieve more success, there are **FREE BONUS RESOURCES** for you at:

YourBonusGift.com

FREE SOCIAL MEDIA CONTENT PLUS
A FREE SOCIAL MEDIA TRAINING DAY VIDEO
which is part of Hank and Sharyn's very successful entrepreneurial marketing program:

The Small Business
MARKETING PLAN
.COM

The Small Business Marketing Plan is a new type of hybrid do-It-Yourself WITH Coaching program that allows small business owners like you to learn the right way to promote their business and increase sales. It begins with teaching you how to create your ideal target market and then speak to them the right way. **The Social Media Training Day** video is a bonus offered to business owners who invest in their business with the Plan. And now it is being given to YOU.

FREE $1997 VALUE

Get started now at

YourBonusGift.com

27

THE SECRETS of SOCIAL MEDIA to BUILD BUSINESS

"Share This Book"

From the creators of *The Small Business Marketing Plan*

The Hows and Whys of Social Media

The **MARKETING CHECKLIST 3**

Includes: A Full Year of Social Media Content PLUS video training for Your Business

Your Extra FREE Bonus Gift ($997 value) YourBonusGift.com

Hank & Sharyn Yuloff

Retail $14.95

Special Quantity Discounts

5-20 Books	$13.95
21-99 Books	$11.50
100-499 Books	$10.25
500-999 Books	$8.95
1000+ Books	$6.95

To Place Your Order Contact:
(800)705-4265
Info@YuloffCreative.com
www.Yuloff Creative .com

Fifty-two Weeks of Memes for Your Social Media

So, what's the deal about memes and why have I given you so many? It's a humorous image, video, piece of text, etc., that is copied (often with slight variations) and spread rapidly by internet users.

Here is your year's worth of social media content. We have created the memes for you and you can capture them at www.YourBonusGift.com. We will also give you far more content there. They are in JPG format and are easy to download and post on your newsfeeds. There is enough content for you to post once a day per business day. We think that as you get used to posting this content, you will begin to post *more* content that you have created.

Will people think "that looks familiar," or, "have I seen someone else use it?" Maybe, but there are hundreds of millions of people using social media in the United States alone, so the odds of them buying this book and using this content are pretty unlikely. But we certainly thank you for assuming our book sales will be *that* high. We expect to be adding far more content on that site, so you will have a huge variety of content to choose from.

We have also added a surprise to that website: a full day *Social Media Training Day* video. We created a marketing program called The Small Business Marketing Plan, which is a do-it-yourself *with coaching* program and this six-hour video series is a small part of it. The Small Business Marketing Plan shows small business owners how to create a marketing plan and gives them the ability to ask questions. This makes it far more than "shelf help." You can see how that works at www.TheSmallBusinessMarketingPlan.com/preview

What is the most important question to ask during a parent/teacher conference?

What words would you use to describe your personal philosophy

How should technology be used to educate children?

What question should every bride and groom should ask each other before the ceremony?

What is your favorite sandwhich?

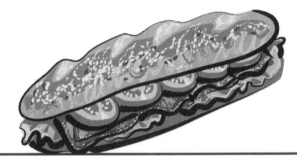

What are a few fun things you love to do?

What do you want to learn about?

Why should we study history?

What do you daydream about?

#OKLNFB

What is the most EPIC THING you have seen in a movie?

#OKLNFB

Has a dream ever changed how you think about something?

What TV show (past or present) would you watch... if it included full nudity?

Which movies can you watch over, and over and over, and.....

#OKLNFB

What would you NOT want to find in your partner's bedside drawer?

#OKLNFB

How would you describe your taste in home decoration?

#OKLNFB

Think back to when you were little. Do you remember how adults described what God looks like?

#OKLNFB

37

If you could be 'The Best' at something, what would choose?

#OKLNFB

AFTER _____

#OKLNFB

38

What is
NOT
a good thing
to bring to
Show-and-Tell?

#OKLNFB

How old were
you when you
had your first
boy/girlfriend?

#OKLNFB

What is one of your favorite books?

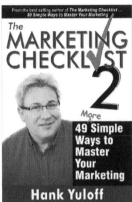

#OKLNFB

PADDED _____

#OKLNFB

CHEESE _____

What is something you would love to do every day of your life?

What is an instant "Mood Killer?"

What is something you hated to be asked when you were younger?

_____ Pie

Would you rather be the worst player on a great team or the best player on a terrible team?

If you were a
professional
wrestler, what
would be your
ring name?

Game _____

44

What are your 5 favorite songs right now?

Nothing tastes or feels as good as _____

What was the last concert you went to?

GOLD ___

OPEN _____

What is your favorite type of music?

Jazz, Rap, Funk, Classic rock, Classical, Disco, Pop, Hip Hop, A Capella, Blues, Rockabilly, Opera, Elevator, Polka, Reggae, RnB, Jingles, Country, Techno, Folk, New Age, Grunge, Metal, Punk...

Quote one of your favorite song lyrics?

#OKLNFB

What song can you just NOT get out of your head?

#OKLNFB

48

What song do you listen to EVERY DAY?

#OKLNFB

What is the most played song on your music player? (iTunes etc)

#OKLNFB

49

_____ up

#OKLNFB

What is in your recipe for happiness?

#OKLNFB

Who would be on your guest list at your dream dinner party?

#OKLNFB

What are the most essential things in your wardrobe?

#OKLNFB

Your Logo Here

51

Do You Believe in Fate?

#OKLNFB

What disease do you think the US Government should focus on curing? (get specific)

#OKLNFB

What board game do you LOVE?

#OKLNFB

What color do you think I should color my hair?

#OKLNFB

What was the worst job you ever had?

#OKLNFB

Do you see yourself as an
a. Optimist
b. Pessimist
c. Realist
d. Generalist
e. Politician

#OKLNFB

54

What is your favorite childhood memory?

How will you spend your 100th birthday?

What 3 things do you think we have in common?

#OKLNFB

What foods would you pack for your ideal picnic basket?

#OKLNFB

Do you let your pet sleep with you?

What would you rather have named after you:
a) a Sandwich at your favorite restaurant.
b) a Holiday.
c) a Chevrolet.
d) a Statue.
e) Something else.

Are you a wine lover?

#OKLNFB

Is there a song which makes you think of your parents?

#OKLNFB

What was your first accomplishment that made you proud of yourself?

#OKLNFB

_____ Power

#OKLNFB

59

Would you break the law to save a loved one from going to jail for 5 years? What went into your decision?

#OKLNFB

I AM one of those people that _____

#OKLNFB

60

What's something you have done that you are reasonably confident you're the only one in my friends list who's done that?

#OKLNFB

What have you seen while driving that has made you laugh or shake your head in amazement?

#OKLNFB

On which magazine cover does your photo belong?

What are some words which are only used in advertisements?

Here is one: quench.

How many cities have you lived in and which has been your favorite?

What is your favorite "ME TIME" thing to do?

What was the
subject of your
biggest
"No Questions
Asked"
favor request?

On which show do
you most want to
appear:
Match Game,
Jeopardy,
Wheel of Fortune
or
The Price is Right?

I went on this one date once and goodness, you will not believe what happened...

What is your favorite type of movie?
a) Comedy
b) Horror
c) Musical
d) Romance
e) Documentary

Are there things your spouse, significant other, partner, best friend.... Does **NOT** know about you?

PARENTS: What is one parenting "tool" or "technique" that has worked well for you with kids?

What song
always makes
you sad?
Why?

#OKLNFB

One ___

#OKLNFB

What song would your friends be surprised to find on your MP3?

Badly Explain Your Profession

You get to
read the
mind of
THREE
PEOPLE.

CLICK

Who are
they?

#OKLNFB

Did you know (you
may have forgotten,
but **THEN**) the name
of each person you
have made
out with?

#OKLNFB

Would you rather have an extra:
a) eye
b) thumb
c) ear
d) toe

Without saying your age, what is something you remember from your childhood that a younger person would not understand?

Scroll down and give me ONE name of a hilarious comedian.

Try not to duplicate

Which is easiest for you to live without for a week:

a) Running Water
b) Electricity
c) Windows

Fill in the blank: I WISH _____

#OKLNFB

What is one thing you still want to achieve in this lifetime?

#OKLNFB

72

What is something you are researching now to buy?

When was the last time you played Truth or Dare? (that is... if you dare tell us)

Fill in the blank: The _____

If you were secretly video'd while you sleeping, what would you hope you wouldn't do at night?
a) snore
b) sleepwalk
c) "scratch yourself"
d) talk
e) make a particular kind of sound from a nether region.

zZZ

74

What is your favorite thing to share with a significant other:
a) a bubble bath
b) a Pizza
c) a couples quiz
d) a romantic walk
e) laundry
f) building a piece of furniture from Ikea that was on sale at 40% off

It _____

or

It's _____

What is something you fill with air?

Fill in the blank

Get _____

What is something a member of the opposite sex (or same sex) can wear that you think is sexy?

#OKLNFB

Who is the TV or Movie Parent you want to be most like?

#OKLNFB

Who was your first celebrity crush? Have one now?

#OKLNFB

Who was your first celebrity crush? Have one now?

#OKLNFB

What is something your child might have in his/her dorm room that you would object to:
a) A professor
b) A Keg
c) A more extensive collection of porn than at home
d) their own pot plant
e) Other

If a man is in training for marriage, what's a word or phrase he should practice saying?
a) I love you
b) I'm so sorry
c) I do
d) Yes, dear
e) OTHER -

WOULD YOU RATHER:

Do all the shopping
for your house
every day for a month
OR
answer EVERY
WHY question from
a 5-year-old for
an hour a day for
a week?

Fill in the blank:

Keep _____

Fill in the blank:

Up _____

What percentage of your friendships began because you worked together?

How do you boost your confidence?

What one species of animal would you most want to be able to communicate with?

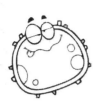

Would you like to be able to make yourself as small as a bacteria? Or as big as a blue whale?

#OKLNFB

What is your favorite color M&M? Peanut or Plain?

Oh... and did you know that M&M's actually stands for "Mars & Murrie's," the last names of the candy's founders.

#OKLNFB

83

Fill in the blank:

Blue __

What song would we be surprised that you know all the words?

Ever taken a road trip by yourself?

Would you rather be transported permanently 500 years in to the future,
or
500 years into the past?

Fill in the blank:

Cold ___

What is your favorite movie or TV show with the name of a city, state, or country in the title?

What is your favorite Song, Album, or Musical Group with the name of a city, state, or country in the title?

#OKLNFB

Fill in the blank:

First _____

#OKLNFB

87

What is the
most odd place
you ever met
someone you
ended up being
'exclusive' with?

Fill in the blank:

Big ____

88

I've been told I was nuts. Many times. If you were going to see a shrink, who would you want it to be?

(Does NOT have to be a SHRINK - pick ANYONE)

#OKLNFB

What is your first memory of your parents?

#OKLNFB

If you were in a witness protection program, what would be your alias?
Your name?
Desired job?

If you had to marry your partner where you met them, where would that be?

Fill in the blank

For _____

What do you think would be the most silly or bizarre thing someone would type into the Google search engine?

Without repeating
someone else's song -

What is your
**FAVORITE
ROCK BALLAD**
of all time?

I'll start:
Don't Stop Believin'
by Journey

#OKLNFB

Describe the color
yellow to somebody
who's blind.

#OKLNFB

Which of these magical lands would you like to take your vacation:

A) Wonderland (to visit Alice and the White Rabbit)

B) Neverland (to visit Tinkerbell)

C) Oz (to follow the Yellow Book Road)

D) Narnia (to visit.... oh heck - none of you are voting for this one)

E) Wherever the Tardis takes you

F) Santa's Workshop at the North Pole

G) Sedona Marketing Retreats
   (pick this one and get $1000
      off next year's bookings)

#OKLNFB

How Often Do You Dance?

#OKLNFB

Fill in the blank

Don't ___

Would you rather be able to reverse one decision you make every day or be able to stop time for 60 seconds every day?

What would you LOVE to have written on a t-shirt?

My Clients All Wanna Hug Me!

Yuloff Creative.com

Fill in the blank

ALL _____

95

When do you think 'childhood' officially ends?

#OKLNFB

Fill in the blank

Make _____

#OKLNFB

What is something that always makes you feel better?

You've been kidnapped. You can call on the characters from one TV show to make a rescue attempt. Which show do you pick?

What was a favorite MOVIE you saw as a child?

#OKLNFB

What is a quality you most admire in others?

#OKLNFB

98

What was your favorite TV show as a child?

Fill in the blank

Go _____

What is your favorite word in a language which is not your primary language?

#OKLNFB

Your choice of a 5-MINUTE QUICKIE today:

A) Sex
B) Getting through your email
C) Your work day
D) Any household chore (ps - sex is NOT a chore)
E) Doing your taxes

#OKLNFB

What APP or APPS on your phone do you check EVERY DAY?

Fill in the blank

IN _____

or

In the _____

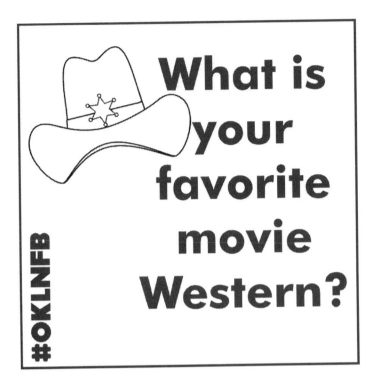

What is your favorite movie Western?

Fill in the blank

_____ Yourself

(keep it clean!)

How do YOU deal with the anniversary of the passing of a loved one?

What is your favorite late evening snack?

Any particular reason or utilization?

Which is your current favorite Sci-Fi series?

Fill in the blank

To ___

Name a T.V. show or Movie with a color in the name? (Example: Blue Lagoon or Blue Bloods)

#OKLNFB

Would You rather have:

A Helper Monkey
or a
Human-like
Robot
or a
British Butler

#OKLNFB

What is the recipe to build your favorite hamburger? Is it something you make at home or get in a restaurant?

#OKLNFB

It's Saturday night.
You're at home... alone.
There is a knock on the door...
You look through the peep hole and **GOODNESS**....

It's your favorite movie character!!!

Who is at the door?

#OKLNFB

Who do you consider a role model?

Do you want to be considered a role model?

By who?

#OKLNFB

What is your ideal dream personalized license plate?
(remember... it's only 7 characters)

#OKLNFB

Describe the worst job you ever had...

What is the best place for chips and salsa? And is the rest of their food any good?

When leaving the house, do you tell your pets when you will return?

The electrician says that for a week, you can only have THREE things plugged in....

What would they be??

From the safety of an alien spacecraft that picked you up: Would you rather go back in time and experience **The Beginning of Planet Earth** or move forward in time and witness **The End of Planet Earth**?

#OKLNFB

Describe your worst date ever....

#OKLNFB

Describe your first date ever....

What is the best compliment you could give to a child?? SHARE IT PLEASE!

You are so SMART!

Describe your HIGH SCHOOL SELF in 6 words

(or less, obviously if you were a "Teacher's Pet")

Which would you pick:

a) Being world-class attractive,

b) A genius,

c) Unbelievably rich, or

d) Famous for doing something great?

Let's see what kind of list we can create... The topic:

WHAT DOES EVERYONE LIKE?

I'll start:
Warm Chocolate Chip cookies

CLICK LIKE on all of the things on the list! (you might want to come back later and read the list)

#OKLNFB

Let's see what kind of list we can create... The topic:

WHAT DO YOU DO?

Add a SHORT description, plus a link to your website.

CLICK LIKE on at least one other person's link and check them out (you might want to come back later and read the list)

#OKLNFB

Someone you've been dating casually (ok... or your spouse) calls and says,

"We have a GREAT weekend ahead of us. Be outside the house in 20 minutes. Oh, and pack for a plane ride."

DO YOU? or DON'T YOU?

What is one thing you would most like to find in a box of Cracker Jack (tm)?

In a LIFE DRAWING class would you rather be:
1) A participant drawing the model.
2) The model.
3) The teacher.
4) The on-call lighting director fom the A/V club.

#OKLNFB

There have been hundreds of them...
All portraying saintly work.

Nurses on Television!

Who is your favorite one (or two) of them?

#OKLNFB

There have been hundreds of them... All portraying life saving work.

Doctors on Television!

Who is your favorite one (or two) of them?

If you could ask your pet 3 questions, what would they be?

Time to pick an
ALL-DEAD ALL-STAR TEAM.
Who is your all star team
made up of:
**1 Dead Singer,
1 Dead Comedian, and
1 Dead Politician?**

My list is at the
top of the comment list.

#OKLNFB

I know y'all love chocolate...
EVERYONE loves chocolate...
BUT....

What do you think is
THE best thing
MADE of Chocolate?

#OKLNFB

117

What is your favorite type of weather?

#OKLNFB

Let's see what kind of list we can create... The topic:

You will LOVE my friend's business!

Add a SHORT description of their company, plus a link to their website.

CLICK LIKE on at least one other person's link and check them out (you might want to come back later and read the list)

#OKLNFB

What was the last dare you accepted?

(If it's been awhile, I DARE you to answer this question while you are naked)

#OKLNFB

Did you ever get caught doing "the sexy stuff" somewhere you were not supposed to be?

#OKLNFB

119

Where is the place you want to take a road trip?

#OKLNFB

What wives tale or conspiracy theory do you think is most likely true?

#OKLNFB

Would you rather your child be accepted by:

a) Hogwarts,
b) The Night's Watch,
c) The Rebel Alliance
   fighter pilot training
or
d) Star Fleet Academy...

And would You let them go?

#OKLNFB

Frankly my dear, I'd like to know...

What is one of your favorite movie quotes?

#OKLNFB

Many people love the song "Its Raining Men" but if the song was about what women REALLY want, it would be called "It's Raining _____"

What would your license plate say, if, that is, it was saying the truth about you?

We are thinking of offering each of you $1 million.

But you have to work at McDonalds for a year and ONLY eat their food.

Are you in?

#OKLNFB

Fill in the blank

HEART ___

#OKLNFB

123

What is your favorite sauce and spices?

What is your favorite place in your home?

124

While many believe Hydrox cookies are an Oreo knock-off, Hydrox actually came first—in 1908, four years before the Oreo.

What is your favorite kind of cookie?

#OKLNFB

"Jay" used to be slang for "foolish person." So when a pedestrian ignored street signs, he was referred to as a "jaywalker."

What is the most useless ticket you have received from the constabulary?

#OKLNFB

The little BIC pen logo guy has a name. It's BIC Boy. Sorry if that's a let down.

Do you have a favorite company logo?

The Small Business
MARKETING✓PLAN

The same person who sang "You're a Mean One, Mr. Grinch" was also the voice of Tony the Tiger (Thurl Ravenscroft)

Do you have a favorite voice on television or advertisement?

The sum of all the numbers on a roulette wheel is 666.

What is your favorite casino game of chance?

#OKLNFB

In the early stage version of The Wizard of Oz, Dorothy's faithful companion Toto was replaced by a cow named Imogene.

Who is your favorite W of O character?

#OKLNFB

127

If you could personally witness anything in history, what would it be?

(for example, the signing of the Declaration of Independence, the first Playboy photo shoot, Guttenberg printing his first Bible, Pompeii being buried by Mount Vesuvius)

Land ho!

#OKLNFB

Did you ever get caught doing "the sexy stuff" somewhere you were not supposed to be?

#OKLNFB

What have you, surprisingly, never tried?

#OKLNFB

If you could make one thing grow on trees
(besides money) what would it be?

#OKLNFB

129

What is something you would **LOVE** to know about that one particular neighbor... you know... **THAT** neighbor...?

YOUNG _____

Would you rather
live without
MUSIC
or
TELEVISION?

Do you take the shampoos and conditioner bottles from a hotel?

Are you afraid of heights? How close to the edge of a drop off would you get?

#OKLNFB

If you could only eat ONE vegetable for the rest of your life it would

be _____

#OKLNFB

132

This is the first thing you see through the window early in the morning...

#OKLNFB

What Do You Do?

Do you press the LEFT button, and receive an INSTANT $1 MILLION or the RIGHT button for a 50% CHANCE or $100 MILLION?

(btw - for those of you who want to press both at the same time, it locks you out of the game, and the floor you are standing on opens, dropping you into a pit of snakes ..... why does it always have to be snakes)

#OKLNFB

Instant Million

50/50 Chance at $100 Million

133

If you could win
any award what
would it be, why?

#OKLNFB

What do you
think of
when I say....
CALIFORNIA?

#OKLNFB

#OKLNFB

You've just won this car!
Keep it? '
Or Sell it?

#OKLNFB

Is this Holiday House...
A) too much
B) not enough
C) I want to do this at our house
D) makes me glad I live
 in an apartment
E) _____

Would you rather find out your parents
are secretly spies for a country unfriendly
to your home country (hey, we have friends
all around the globe)...

OR

are aliens from a
planet in a galaxy
far far away and
you are adopted
(think MiB)?

#OKLNFB

Would you rather spend a year
on the International Space Station
and not be able to have sex,
OR,
a year submerged on a submarine
with your significant other (where
we assume, you **WILL** be able
to have sex)?

#OKLNFB

Who's Autograph would you like to get on a photo of you and them? (Living Celebrity or famous Person)

#OKLNFB

Write the happiest story you can... using only 4 words.

#OKLNFB

You are at a social event. Music's jumping. Bass is pumping. You start tapping your foot. You are READY TO DANCE ... You spy the DJ running the music....

#OKLNFB

WHAT SONG ARE YOU GOING TO ASK HER TO PLAY?

#OKLNFB

Did you ever get a gift that you'd still like to return? Anything you want to donate to the Universe? Have any "Wishes for the World" for the next 12 months?

What could a psychic tell you (or HAS a psychic told you) that you would (did) absolutely 100% believe?

#OKLNFB

What is the most bizaar (other than these, perhaps) flavor of potato chips that you can imagine wanting to try?

#OKLNFB

Have you ever run out one cleaning product and switched out another cleaning product that is supposed to be used for something else?

#OKLNFB

What could they put on sale that is so great, you buy 60 of them??

#OKLNFB

What is that **ONE** (ok, maybe two) quintessential album, which when you first heard it made you say
"WHOA!"

Which of these did you use last?
A) Yellow Pages book (not as a doorstop!)
B) a call to 411 information
C) a public coin operated phone
D) a fax machine
E) a VCR

For some it's "Let it Go" from Frozen and "YMCA" from the Village People. What is one of those songs that just makes you **CRINGE** each time it infests your audio canal?

#OKLNFB

What is the punch line of your favorite joke?

Knock Knock Jokes

#OKLNFB

142

If someone paid you a $1 Million to get a tattoo of a song title...

What tattoo would you choose and where would you put it?

#OKLNFB

Think of a country you have always wanted to travel to. Your favorite airlines has just announced a round-trip fare of $2 due to an dysentery outbreak. "

Would you travel to your dream destination?

#OKLNFB

143

We can tell it's the beginning of the Holiday Season when its time for Pumpkin Spice EVERYTHING. WHAT IS YOUR FAVORITE PUMPKIN SPICE THING???

#OKLNFB

We all know that the US Secret Service has code names for the people they protect. If you became a protected individual, what would you like your code name to be?

#OKLNFB

Classical, comedy, political, poetry slam, rock, speech, science lecture.....
What is your favorite type of concert to attend?

#OKLNFB

Your BEST friend has been arrested and WRONGLY accused of MURDER.... He has left it in YOUR hands to hire the best TELEVISION SERIES LAWYER to defend him.
Which TELEVISION SERIES LAWYER would you hire and why?

#OKLNFB

What is your total?

1. HAD SEX: $10.00
2. SMOKED: $3.00
3. GOT DRUNK: $7.00
4. WENT SKINNY DIPPING: $5.00
5. KISSED SOMEONE OF THE OPPOSITE SEX: $5.00
6. KISSED SOMEONE OF THE SAME SEX: $5.00
7. CHEATED ON A TEST: $2.00
8. FELL ASLEEP IN CLASS $0.50
9. BEEN EXPELLED: $5.00
10. BEEN IN A FIST FIGHT: $10.00
11. STOLE SOMETHING: $2.00
12. DONE DRUGS: $5.00
13. DYED YOUR HAIR: $0.50
14. CRIED YOURSELF TO SLEEP: $1.00
15. BEEN IN LOVE: $4.00
16. GOT CAUGHT DOING SOMETHING THAT YOU SHOULDN'T HAVE BEEN DOING: $1.00
17. WENT STREAKING: $4.00
18. GOT ARRESTED: $5.00
19. MADE OUT WITH SOMEONE: $2.00
20. PEED IN THE POOL: $0.50
21. PLAYED SPIN THE BOTTLE: $1.00
22. DONE SOMETHING YOU REGRET: $3.00

#OKLNFB

From any movie Western, who is your favorite cowboy hero?

#OKLNFB

Time to play "Would you rather?"

A Be able to read minds
B Fly
C Become a dragon
D Talk to animals
E Play lead guitar for ZZ Top
F Eat chocolate all day and
　　never gain weight

#OKLNFB

Name a movie title and at the end add... "in my pants."

#OKLNFB

Is bald beautiful?

We spent part of our 25th anniversary in Winslow, Arizona.

Ever been somewhere named in a song?

#OkLateNightFacebookers

What is your favorite place to swim?
a) pool
b) bubbly spa
c) river
d) mountain lake
e) ocean
f) other

What was the name of your childhood teddy bear?
(You can also give us your current bear's moniker)

Favorite Place to buy a pair of jeans?

a) Wal-Mart,
b) Target
c) Kmart
d) Macys
e) Nordstrom
f) other?

#OKLNFB

Which snack is best:
a) Cheetos tm
b) Fritos tm
c) Peanuts
d) sunflower seeds
e) other

#OKLNFB

What kind of school contest did you win? (spelling bee, election, sports ribbon)

#OKLNFB

Ever had a crush on one of your teachers? A boss? A friend's sibling?

#OKLNFB

What is your favorite musical?

#OKLNFB

What were some occupations you wanted to be when you were a kid?

#OKLNFB

152

Do you believe in ghosts?

Ever have a Deja-vu feeling?
Ever have a Deja-vu feeling?
Ever have a Deja-vu feeling?
Ever have a Deja-vu feeling?
Ever have a Deja-vu feeling?

Are you stubborn?
Seriously... are you?
ANSWER THE
QUESTION!

#OKLNFB

What is your
astrological
sign?
Bonus points for
the Chinese
sign, too

#OKLNFB

Who is your favorite Late-Night talk show entertainer?

#OKLNFB

Do you sing in the car? Shower?

#OKLNFB

155

How many moving
violations have you
talked your way out
of receiving?

#OKLNFB

Do you always
smile for pictures?

#OKLNFB

smile

156

Do you cut out coupons but then never use them?

#OKLNFB

$50 OFF
Promotional
Product Orders

What is your usual bedtime?

#OKLNFB

What is your favorite food?

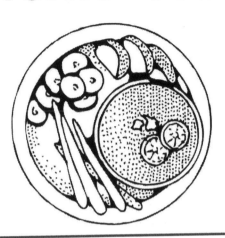

What is your GO-TO Halloween costume?

Have you ever walked out of a movie?

#OKLNFB

Would you rather ...
Have the ability to swap
genders whenever you want
OR
Have the ability to change
your age whenever you want?

#OKLNFB

Want More Training?

No More Business Blinders

Getting You Focused for Success

Hank and Sharyn Yuloff
*share their secrets on how to
create your own marketing plan...*
AND THEY'RE THERE TO COACH YOU!

The Small Business
MARKETING✓PLAN

**The D.I.Y. Marketing Plan
with a Coaching Program**

| Hours of video with a complete action guide that creates your plan. | Private Facebook Group to network and have your questions answered. | PLUS: Your favorite Non-Profit receives a copy of the plan. |

INCLUDES a BONUS 6-HOUR LIVE SOCIAL MEDIA TRAINING VIDEO

Do your business a favor and take the time to enroll now

TheSmallBusinessMarketingPlan.com

Special <u>FREE</u> Bonus Gift for <u>YOU!</u>

To help you achieve more success, there are **FREE BONUS RESOURCES** for you at:

YourBonusGift.com

FREE SOCIAL MEDIA CONTENT PLUS
A FREE SOCIAL MEDIA TRAINING DAY VIDEO

Get started now at

YourBonusGift.com

THE SECRETS of SOCIAL MEDIA to BUILD BUSINESS

"Share This Book"

From the creators of *The Small Business Marketing Plan*

The Hows and Whys of Social Media

The **MARKETING CHECKLIST 3**

Includes:
A Full Year of
Social Media
Content PLUS
video training
for Your
Business

Your Extra
FREE Bonus Gift
($997 value)
YourBonusGift.com

Hank & Sharyn Yuloff

Retail
$14.95

Special Quantity Discounts

5-20 Books	$13.95
21-99 Books	$11.50
100-499 Books	$10.25
500-999 Books	$8.95
1000+ Books	$6.95

To Place Your Order Contact:
(800)705-4265
Info@YuloffCreative.com
www.Yuloff Creative .com